# DEDICATION

To the eternal divine cosmic
energy, the feminine form of
Shakti, Goddess Durga.

May She empower us with Her
divine strength.

When it comes to the authenticity of The Jais Jais retelling of the ancient stories. We have found lots of variations in the original scriptures of the Devi Mahatmya and Puranas, and stories told over time. The stories that we have written may differ to other teachings. We would like to share stories with our children in a fun, vibrant and engaging style …The Jai Jais Way.

Published by The Jai Jais Ltd
Copyright The Jai Jais Ltd
All rights reserved
The Jai Jais is a Registered Trademark of The Jai Jais Ltd
The moral right of the authors and illustrator has been asserted
ISBN 978-1-9163242-9-9

# The Jai Jais®

## Legends Series

# Nine Divine Goddesses of Navratri

by Asmita Bhudia and Sunita Shah

Illustrated by James Ballance

**Om** - a sacred Hindu symbol which represents God and the entire universe. Alternative spelling is Aum.

# Contents:

# INTRODUCTION

The popular festival of Navratri is dedicated to the divine Goddess Durga, who is revered for nine days and nights. In Sanskrit, "Nav" means nine and "ratri" means nights.

"Maa" means mother in Sanskrit, Goddess Durga is the divine mother. Goddess Durga symbolises the divine energy that exists in the entire universe. She is the feminine form of Shakti (power, strength and might).

The Navratri festival is celebrated all over the world by Hindus in many different ways such as Durga pujas, Garba dances and spectacular parades. They all honour Goddess Durga and her divine energies which are intertwined within the whole universe.

The wonderful festival of Navratri is celebrated four times a year. The most popular celebrations are held during Sharad Navratri which takes place in the autumn season during September/October. Chaitra Navratri is remembered in the spring season during March/April which is also celebrated throughout the world.

During each of the nine nights of Navratri festival, Goddess Durga is worshipped in different forms, these are called Navdurga. These nine divine and powerful forms of the mighty and brave Goddess Durga are:

## Maa Shailaputri

## Maa Brahmacharini

## Maa Chandraghanta

## Maa Kushmanda

## Maa Skandamata

## Maa Katyayani

## Maa Kaalratri

## Maa Mahagauri

## Maa Siddhidatri

Her nine divine forms of Navdurga demonstrate important qualities such as patience, intelligence, dedication, determination, justice, strength, self-confidence, resilience and countless others. Goddess Durga inspires her devotees to choose the right paths in their journeys of life. Let's learn about these nine amazing forms of Goddess Durga and She will no doubt inspire you too!

# MAA SHAILAPUTRI

Meaning of Name: The daughter (putri) of the mountain (shaila).

Mantra: Oṃ Devī Shailaputryai Namaḥ

Offerings: Ghee (Clarified butter).

On the first day of Navratri, the goddess Maa Shailaputri is worshipped. Shailaputri means "the daughter of the mountains". She is the daughter of Himavat, the King of the Himalayas. Shailaputri symbolises perseverance and sacrifice.

In her previous life, Shailaputri was born as Sati, the daughter of Daksha Prajapati, who was the son of Lord Brahma. Sati was gentle and kind. She was a purehearted young lady, who was adored by everyone.

Sati and Lord Shiva were very much in love and wanted to get married. Sati underwent many challenges to fulfil her heart's desire. She asked her father for permission to marry Shiva, but to her surprise, Daksha Prajapati replied with a stern and unapproving voice, "My dear daughter Sati, you come from a noble and prestigious family, yet you desire to marry that scruffy and unkept man! It puzzles me how you can choose such a person as your lifelong partner. You are too good for that unrefined Shiva. You do not have my blessings to marry Shiva. I insist that you find a more suitable match with someone more deserving and similar to our status."

A sorrowful Sati pondered on the sharp words of her father. These cruel words distressed her mind. She had already given her heart to Shiva, and there was no one else she wanted to spend the rest of her life with. Upon further contemplation, Sati bravely made a bold decision; she was intent on marrying Lord Shiva and that is exactly what she was going to do!

Sati spoke to her mother, Prasuti, and told her about her determination to marry Shiva. So heartfelt were Sati's words that her mother agreed to the companionship and started to prepare for the wedding. Daksha Prajapati was not at all pleased, he did not like Shiva at all, but reluctantly allowed the marriage to go ahead seeing that there was no way to change his daughter's mind.

When the wedding day finally arrived, everyone was very excited. True to her word, Prasuti organised a magnificent and vibrant wedding for Sati and Shiva in her grand palace. The mandap, wedding canopy, was beautifully decorated with marigold flowers that shone like bright glowing lanterns, and all the royal guests were adorned in their finest clothes to welcome the groom and his wedding procession. The air was filled with joyous love and laughter. Everything was so splendid on this day, the whole kingdom seemed to sparkle like shining gems. Everything that is, except Shiva… and his guests.

Shiva arrived at the grand wedding riding on Nandi, his strong trusted bull. Shiva did not seem to have made any effort with his presentation even on his own wedding day! Shiva's sea blue neck was strung with plain brown Rudraksha beads, and his long hair remained matted like tangles of rugged rope. He simply wore his daily attire of a husky tiger skin tunic.

The groom's procession that accompanied him was a ghoulish and very peculiar crowd. They were also dressed like simpletons in dark and dull clothing, much like the groom. It seemed as though they were certainly out of place for attending such a lavish wedding.

Shiva's wedding procession cheerily arrived whilst loudly beating their drums, and dancing merrily to announce their arrival. Prasuti warmly welcomed Shiva, offering him a colourful garland of fresh flowers. Daksha Prajapati, however, was not so welcoming and begrudgingly invited his future son-in-law to the wedding canopy, without a smile or any warmth. He was in disbelief that a groom and his guests would appear at his palace in unsuitable attire, especially for such an elaborate occasion, his precious daughter's wedding. He was expecting a prince to take his daughter's hand in marriage, not a scruffy man!

The wedding rituals were underway, and melodious chants of Sanskrit mantras echoed around the palace. It was time for the bride to enter the wedding canopy. Sati was the most beautiful bride who dazzled as bright as a diamond. She gracefully stepped into the mandap, and her sparkling eyes met with the love of her life, Shiva. They both knew there was no one else in the entire world they wanted to promise the rest of their lives to.

A grand celebration was underway to rejoice in the union, and all the wedding guests were having the most wonderful time. There was dancing, singing, and the most spectacular feast. The devas (divine beings) in the heavens showered their blessings on the newlyweds, as the confetti of flowers gracefully rained down from the sky.

As the wedding ended, it was time for Sati to say an emotional farewell to her family. Sati accompanied her husband to her new home in Kailash, high in the majestic mountains of the Himalayas.

After a few years of happily married life, Sati heard her father was conducting a Yagna, a ritual to the divine, conducted in front of a sacred fire. She excitedly said, "Oh Shiva, I've heard that my dear father is having a Yagna, let us go there. I do miss my family and friends greatly; it'll be so nice to see them after such a long while."

"My dear, we haven't received an invitation, I do not think that it is appropriate to attend." Shiva gently replied.

Sati chuckled innocently, "Oh my love, they must have overlooked to invite us by mistake. You know how busy palace life can be! After all, a daughter is always welcome to visit her parents' home anytime. Who needs an invitation?!"

Shiva was still unsure and warned her, "My dear, we should await an invitation first."

"Oh noble one, I just simply cannot wait! I will take your leave tomorrow and journey to my parents' home and be witness to their auspicious Yagna," Sati said delicately as she yearned to see her family and friends.

The next day, Sati excitedly left for her parents' palace. After a long journey down from the mountains, she had finally arrived. Her mother embraced and welcomed Sati with open arms. "Oh Mother, how lovely it is to see you again!" expressed Sati. "I've missed you so much."

In the distance, she could see her father who looked enraged and with an uninviting expression on his face. A stern voice bellowed across the palace court, "Sati! What are you doing here?! You made your pledge to be Shiva's wife and left home. You are no longer welcome here anymore, go back there to where you belong!"

Sati was heartbroken by the unexpected spiteful words shouted by her own father. A tiny teardrop left her eye and rolled down her soft, innocent face. She felt ridiculed and humiliated. Daksha Prajapati was not finished embarrassing his daughter, "Look at her, my guests, she came by herself like a lost lamb crawling back to her herd. Obviously, she was too embarrassed to bring her ruffian husband!"

The guests' sharp stares struck Sati like hundreds of deadly daggers, as her father continued to fire arrows of insults and humiliation towards her one true love, Shiva. Sati encountered feelings of torment, anguish, and deep sadness. She felt as though she was completely alone. Nobody could take that agony away. In that moment, no support was given from any of her family or friends, she felt cornered with nowhere to turn. Darkness and negativity engrossed Sati's mind. She couldn't think clearly as Sati was overcome with frantically racing and uncontrollable destructive emotions. Sati could not take it anymore, she wished that she could disappear! She could no longer tolerate the disgrace and insults from her own father, in the presence of all her family and friends.

"For every birth I take, I vow to be Shiva's wife, he will be my one true love for eternity!" Sati firmly swore.

With all hope lost, she did not want to live any longer! Sati did not give a second thought and slowly stepped into the centre of the yagna fire. The court could do nothing but watch in horror as the flames danced around her virtuous body and hastily consumed her.

Though Shiva was far away, the bond of love between them was very strong, he could sense Sati was in trouble. In desperation he raced down from the mountains and rushed into Daksha Prajapati's palace, only to find his gentle wife fading away into the golden glows of the ravaging fire. Without hesitation, Shiva drew out his beloved from the fire but she was no more. As he held lifeless Sati in his arms, grief struck the core of his heart like a poisonous arrow. His fury grew from knowing her death and sorrow were caused by the cruelty of her father. Shiva let out a ferocious roar that quaked and crumbled the palace walls. The mountains trembled in the distance causing devastating avalanches rushing from the high snow-capped Himalayan hills. From Shiva's matted hair came the two ferocious and terrifying forms of Veerabhadra and Bhadrakali.

Veerabhadra and Bhadrakali represent the fierce forces and energies of Shiva and Shakti, which if not controlled can cause immense destruction within the universe. They are essential in keeping a delicate equilibrium that maintains order in the universe.

Veerabhadra's skin was as dark as a thousand thundering clouds. His many arms wielded powerful weapons, and around his neck dangled a garland of skulls. Bhadrakali was fierce, resilient, and ready for battle. She sprouted numerous arms that held impressive weapons such as a shimmering blade, a gruelling gada, a terrifying trishul, and a serrated chakra. Her fearsome form reflected her rage against injustice.

With a mighty swing of his razor-sharp trishul, Veerabhadra destroyed the cruel and egotistical Daksha Prajapati.

Observing the frightful conflict, Lord Vishnu and Lord Brahma intercepted and desperately pleaded with mighty Veerabhadra to calm himself and regain control. After many attempts, the wisdom and strength of these gods finally prevailed, the raging avatars were pacified, and Shiva manifested his original form. Though heartbroken by the loss of his true love, Shiva remained compassionate. He saw Prasuti's sadness from losing her husband, and so restored Daksha Prajapati to life. So that the man would remain humble, when Daksha Prajapati was brought back to life, Shiva replaced his head with that of a goat.

Daksha Prajapati's regrets ran deep; he realised his grave mistake and fell mercifully at Shiva's feet, "My dear son, what has my arrogance done?! No words can express how sorry I am! I beg for your forgiveness! I now understand the dreadful consequences of my inexcusable words and actions."

Shiva graciously pardoned Daksha Prajapati and before leaving the palace, he miraculously restored the damage he had caused in his uncontrollable fierce form. Following the events of that day, Daksha Prajapati became a devoted follower of Lord Shiva.

Many years later, Sati was born again as "Shailaputri," the daughter of the Himalayas. In this incarnation, she was also known as Parvati and Hemavati. She dedicated years of devotion and meditation to Shiva. As she had vowed as Sati, in her next life, she married Lord Shiva as Shailaputri. The two divine beings were united once more.

# MAA BRAHMACHARINI

Meaning of name: "Brahmacharini" means female monk (seeker).
Mantra: Oṃ Devī Brahmachāriṇyai Namaḥ
Offering: Sugar

Maa Brahmacharini is the form of Durga celebrated on the second day of Navratri. She is the symbol of love, sacrifice, dedication, self-confidence and fortitude.

Sati was reborn as the daughter of the mountains known as Parvati. During this birth, she became known as Brahmacharini.

Parvati lived happily as a daughter of King Himavat, the King of Himalaya. When Parvati became a young adult, she was intent on marrying Shiva. As you already know, during her previous birth as Sati, she had made a vow to marry Shiva in her next incarnation.

Now that Sati had been reborn as Parvati, she was determined to fulfil this promise. The maiden Parvati wanted to pursue the path of intense prayer dedicated to Lord Shiva. Her parents advised Parvati against such a challenging and difficult path, but Parvati's mind was made up.

"My dear daughter, Parvati, you are a princess, and you have countless suitors. You do not need to go through so much hardship, trouble, and penance to attain Shiva," cautioned Himavat.

"I must marry Lord Shiva. He is forever in my heart. I will wed no other!" Parvati spoke from her heart.

Determined Parvati decided to leave behind the comforts, riches and splendour of the grand palace. "I am ready to go and live like Lord Shiva, in the high mountains. There, my way of life will be modest and saintly, and I will be in constant prayer and meditation to my Lord." Parvati abandoned all her shining jewellery and transformed herself from a royal princess to a humble maiden, dressed in simple robes. She left her majestic palace and bid farewell to her friends and family.

Parvati's journey was not one for the faint-hearted. She painstakingly trekked a great distance, into the soaring, snow-capped mountains. She eventually found a lonely, peaceful region high up on a mountain peak where Parvati settled down, far away from any distractions. The only sound heard was the cool breeze whispering through the trees. Parvati practised the same spiritual disciplines such as yoga, deep meditation and prayer, just like her inspirational one true love, Lord Shiva.

Many years passed and Parvati continued to remain true to her devotion. She meditated upon Lord Shiva in the icy cold and often treacherous conditions. Snow crystals tumbled all around her, and bitter gusts of wind churned the frosty skies, nonetheless, faithful Parvati still persevered.

Shiva was drawn to her commitment, which sparked his curiosity to find out more. Shiva disguised himself into a human form, to meet Parvati, attempting to divert the path of her devotion, by criticising and mocking himself. "The one that you have chosen to meditate on night and day, is nonsense! Why do you constantly repeat his name? It is gibberish! Shiva is not worthy of praise or even an insult! You are wasting your time and energy with him, putting yourself through such hardship!" Shiva cunningly said to Parvati.

Parvati took no notice of these wasted words uttered by a stranger; she didn't know it was Shiva in disguise. The words travelled through one ear and out the other. Courageously, she continued to focus her mind and thoughts on Lord Shiva. In this part of Parvati's life, she is known as Maa Brahmacharini.

Many more years passed; Parvati continued her spiritual disciplines and she had become very thin due to lack of nutrition. She was weak and frail, the shadow she cast on the ground was so faint. The former princess no longer resembled royalty; her body had withered away like a wrinkled flower. However, this did not deter her at all. She was so strong-willed, nothing could stop her from reaching her goal, and that was Lord Shiva.

One day, an evil demon by the name of Prachandasura and his large army launched an unexpected and vicious attack on innocent Parvati. She had reached the final phase of her meditation and was near to completion. Having seen helpless Parvati unaware of the imminent attack, Goddess Lakshmi and Goddess Saraswati felt compelled to come to her aid. Using their special powers, Goddess Lakshmi and Goddess Saraswati guarded and protected Parvati. The number of demons were too many for them to control.

After numerous days of battle, Parvati's waterpot had been knocked over and fell to the icy floor. Parvati's powerful penance transformed the falling water droplets into a huge gushing flood, which carried the demon army away in its rough and turbulent waters.

All the commotion caused by Prachandasura disturbed Parvati who awoke from her deep meditation. Parvati had developed immense inner strength during her countless years of prayer and deep meditation. She deliberately opened her intense eyes and immediately caught sight of the wicked Prachandasura. Parvati's powerful lightning gaze instantaneously turned him into a pile of ashes.

Everyone in the cosmos was fascinated by Goddess Parvati's meditation and dedication to Lord Shiva.

Having heard about Parvati's achievements, Shiva once again decided to pay her a visit in another disguise, that of a Brahmachari, a male monk. Adorned in a simple orange robe, he quizzed Parvati with complicated riddles. Without any hesitation, Parvati presented accurate answers to every single question. Their interesting and detailed philosophical conversation continued for days, and Parvati proved her intelligence and wisdom to Shiva's charade.

The Brahmachari proudly announced to Parvati with a mischievous smile, "I am impressed by your devotion and knowledge. You are suited to me, for I am also wise and ingenious much like yourself!" He mystically transformed himself to his normal form as Lord Shiva, with his iconic blue skin, his neck embellished with rudraksha beads and a snake garland, dressed in a golden tiger skin, his crescent moon adorning his matted hair, carrying his mighty Trishul weapon. In her humble form of a female monk, Brahmacharini Parvati was amazed. "I have waited countless years to meet you, My Lord Shiva! It will be my utmost honour to marry you!"

Brahmacharini Parvati finally completed her many years of meditation and spiritual practices. She returned home to her beloved parents and informed them of her success. Proud Himavat declared, "Parvati, your penance, love and dedication to your Lord Shiva are genuinely admirable and truly inspirational. It will be our greatest honour to arrange your wedding celebrations. You will continue to inspire for generations to come."

An extravagant wedding took place. The whole kingdom was invited to witness the auspicious marriage of Lord Shiva and Goddess Parvati. It was truly a joyous and memorable occasion for all!

DAY THREE:

# MAA CHANDRAGHANTA

Meaning of name: "Chandra" means moon and "ghanta" means bell.
Mantra: Oṃ Devī Chandraghaṇṭāyai Namaḥ
Offering: Rice pudding (Kheer)

Maa Chandraghanta is a form of Durga celebrated on the third day of Navratri. She is the symbol of equality, empathy and intelligence. Maa Chandraghanta is known to remove negative energies and provides inspiration during challenging times. She blesses devotees with divine grace and courage.

The name Chandraghanta comes from two Sanskrit words: "Chandra" which means "moon," and "Ghanta" which means "bell". She adorns a special tilak on her forehead with a half-moon that is shaped like a bell. There is an interesting legend behind this form of Maa Chandraghanta.

When Sati was reborn as Goddess Parvati, she devoted herself to many years of unwavering devotion to Lord Shiva, in the form of Maa Brahmacharini. Having attained her heart's desire, Parvati approached her father, Himavat. "Oh, dear father, I have dedicated so many years of devotion, meditation and gruelling penance to attain my Lord Shiva, and now I finally have gained my one true love. We wish to marry; we both want to spend the rest of our lives with each other."

"Oh my dear daughter Parvati, I am so proud of you. The whole world praises your dedication and determination. You will continue to inspire for generations to come. It will be my greatest honour to organise your wedding celebrations," joyfully replied Himavat, King of Himalaya.

King Himavat and Queen Mainavati organised a grand and magnificent wedding for their daughter. The majestic Himalayan kingdom, adorned with bright and beautiful décor, was ready to welcome Shiva and his guests. Colourful fragrant flowers gently scattered around the kingdom and palace; the air was filled with fun and laughter. The wedding mandap was delicately decorated with sparkling diamonds that mirrored the snowdrops in the distant hills.

The joyous occasion had arrived, and the whole kingdom was excited about the grand affair. Dressed in their finest clothes, the citizens eagerly awaited the groom's wedding procession.

In the distant mountain path, the peaks echoed the joyful beating of drums and cheerful singing of groomsmen. Shiva's wedding procession was on its way to the wedding venue.

As they approached the palace, King Himavat and Queen Mainavati caught a glimpse of their future son-in-law and his guests. They were both utterly shocked to see Shiva descend with a huge yet extremely unusual wedding procession on his own wedding day. This peculiar pageant included ghosts, sages, goblins and ghouls. Queen Mainavati was completely baffled, her eyes suddenly froze at seeing this unbelievable mockery of a wedding procession. Lord Shiva was covered in cloudy grey ash, with a scaly cobra snake coiled around his sea blue neck. His lengthy, twisted and tangled hair was half tied effortlessly with a string of grainy brown Rudraksha mala beads. Lord Shiva was not the vision of a traditional handsome groom.

Lord Shiva, also known as Mahadev, had many devotees from many different backgrounds. The devas (divine beings) as well as asuras (creatures of lower nature) such as ghosts and ghouls, worshipped him too. Lord Shiva never discriminated between his devotees, all of them were equally important. He treated the devas, asuras and all other creatures fairly and always attempted to guide them to the path of righteousness and Dharma. So, all these different groups of devotees were welcome to join Shiva's wedding procession.

However, not fully understanding this, the frightening appearance alarmed the family and friends of King Himavat, especially Queen Mainavati who swiftly fainted at the bewildering sight of this eerie procession.

Parvati, embellished with a beautiful and delicate embroidered saree, was the most beautiful bride. She wore jewels and diamonds which sparkled against the backdrop of the glistening snow-white mountains. From the corner of her twinkling eye, Parvati caught sight of Lord Shiva's scary and unusual wedding procession from her balcony.

When she witnessed Shiva's strange wedding procession and his form, Parvati didn't find him any different from his other appearances. Shiva was the love of her life, no matter how he appeared. She was deeply in love with his blissful divinity and kind personality, not with the way Shiva looked. She looked through his outwardly appearance and knew the Lord that he was underneath.

Parvati decided to magically transform herself to equally match the form of her future husband. She took the spellbinding form of Chandraghanta. Parvati's usual golden complexion transformed into a dark tone like dusky thunderclouds. Her gentle eyes turned into a fierce gaze. She developed ten mighty arms, some of which were adorned with powerful weapons such as a trishul, an arrow, a bow, a gada, a sword, and a spear. She carried a lotus flower, a bell, and a water pot. Her tenth hand was open-palmed, always ready to gracefully shower blessings on her devotees. This majestic form of Chandraghanta was riding on a fearless, golden mighty lion. In the form of Maa Chandraghanta, Parvati equalled the Shakti of Lord Shiva. This is where she is known as Adi Shakti.

From the corner of his eye, Shiva caught the gaze of Parvati's very frightening and intimidating form of Chandraghanta. Much to his amazement, the traditional bride that he expected had transformed into an all-powerful warrior goddess. Even though no words were spoken, Shiva immediately understood Parvati's wishes. He mystically transformed himself into a handsome and charming groom who was impeccable and flawless. Now, Shiva's hair was neatly tied back, and his face gleamed with a handsome smile. The snake coiled around his neck had transformed into a beautiful flower garland.

Queen Mainavati regained her consciousness and she felt as though she had a nightmare! "I thought I saw a scary ghoul asking for the hand of my precious and beautiful daughter! I am so happy to know that this wild hallucination is over!"

Queen Mainavati now set her eyes on a striking groom, which she thought was more suited for her daughter. The elaborate and vibrant wedding ceremonies were now underway.

Lord Shiva and Goddess Parvati's glamorous marriage took place with the chanting of melodious prayers and rituals. The marriage of this divine couple was jubilantly celebrated all over the kingdom and world. Joyful singing and dancing, as well as delicious feasting, was enjoyed by all the guests. From this day forward, the occasion is celebrated as Maha Shivaratri.

# MAA KUSHMANDA

Meaning of name: "Ku" means little,  "Ushma" means warmth or energy and "Anda" means egg.

Mantra: Oṃ Devī Kūṣmāṇḍāyai Namaḥ

Offerings: Milk and halwa (sweet)

Maa Kushmanda is a form of Durga celebrated on the fourth day of Navratri. She is known as the smiling goddess. Her name consists of three parts; 'Ku' means little, 'Ushma' means smiling or warmth and 'Anda' means egg. She symbolises creativity and ingenuity.

In this form, Maa Kushmanda is the creator. The craftsperson of the entire Universe and all of creation within. She is the "Divine Mother of the Universe". There are many different legends associated with creation, here is Maa Kushmanda's legend.

At the beginning of time, there was nothing. The universe was non-existent. The infinite space was immersed with unlimited darkness which had no beginning or end. A pitch-black wilderness of nothing. It was still, silent, without life. A mysterious empty canvas, with no form or shape, simply timeless.

Suddenly, a blinding luminous ray of divine light appeared, illuminating every corner of this abyss, wondrously dispelling all darkness. Initially, this divine light was formless. The bright fluorescent light softly mellowed to paint the infinite sky with a vibrant rainbow spectrum.

Soon, the divine light clustered in one area and it started taking an elegant shape which finally manifested itself in the form of a gracious and divine lady. This celestial lady, the first being in the entire Universe was Maa Kushmanda.

Maa Kushmanda's magnificent form consisted of a divine lady with eight mighty arms. In her hands, she carried impressive weapons such as a mighty bow, a razor-sharp arrow, a dynamic chakra and a formidable gada. She also held a simple kamandal (a small pot), a pure lotus flower and a mala. Her kamandal contained the nectar of immortality called amrit. Her trusted vehicle was a ferocious and fearless lion.

Maa Kushmanda's mystical energy sculpted planets, galaxies and stars, and scattered them into the infinite blue sky. Soon after, with the brilliance of her loving smile, she miraculously created the sun. It began to glow as a beacon of light to the rest of the solar system. Her divine energy strengthened the sun and illuminated the sky radiantly, giving warmth and light with its celestial rays, thus Surya was born.

She gently guided the shining Surya to move and spin in the right direction and to hold the planets of the solar system in their orbits. The canvas of the cosmos was now complete.

Maa Kushmanda divinely created three new life forms from her own energy. She created the powerful Mahakali from her left eye. Mahakali was a fierce and strong goddess. Maa Kushmanda's right eye created the gracious and wise Mahasaraswati. From the centre of her forehead, the third spiritual eye, she created Mahalakshmi.

The three equally magnificent creations from Maa Kushmanda's divine shakti, each continued the craft of creation. The body of Mahakali gave birth to a male named Shiva, and a female, Saraswati. Similarly, Mahalakshmi also gave birth to a male named Brahma and a female called Lakshmi. Maa Kushmanda then glimpsed at Mahasaraswati, who then gave birth to a male, Vishnu, and a female, Parvati. The mighty six were formed!

After these wonderful and miraculous creations, Maa Kushmanda ingeniously offered companions to each of them. Saraswati was paired with Brahma; Lakshmi was matched with Vishnu and Parvati was accompanied with Shiva.

Mahakali, Mahasaraswati and Mahalakshmi became mystically immersed in their original source of the Supreme Goddess, Maa Kushmanda. She majestically transformed herself into a source of divine energy which became infused within her magnificent creation of the Universe, like a thread supporting beads on a necklace. She is the Shakti that is needed in all living forms as a source of life and energy. Her name Kushmanda suggests that she is the creator of this "little cosmic egg", that is known as our Universe. With a calm smile by the divine Goddess, Maa Kushmanda powerfully created more divine light and weaved her magical energy into every fabric of creation.

# MAA SKANDAMATA

Meaning of name: "Skandamata" means "the mother of Skanda".

Mantra: Oṃ Devī Skandamātāyai Namaḥ

Offering: Bananas.

Maa Skandamata is worshipped on the fifth day of Navratri. "Skanda" is the first-born child of Shiva and Parvati, he is also known as "Kartikeya" and "Murugan". "Mata" means mother. Skandamata translates as the "Mother of Skanda". In this form, she is a guiding light and an empowering mother.

From previous legends, after the unexpected and challenging death of his beloved wife Sati, Shiva became very disconnected from the world. He absorbed himself in penance and deep meditation, detached from everyone and everything. During this time, there lived an evil asura named Tarakasura. He had received a boon that only the child of Shiva and Parvati can destroy him. Malicious Tarakasura was overjoyed when he heard about the death of innocent Sati, and he thought himself to be invincible.

"I am the most powerful asura, and I am now immortal. Shiva is overcome with grief due to Sati's death. He is useless, with no motivation to do anything. No more Sati means no child of Shiva! I am protected as no one can ever destroy me!" he claimed with a wicked cackle. Cunning Tarakasura caused havoc and misery, terrorising heaven and earth. He continuously attacked the worlds and looted the luxurious wealth of the devas. The defenceless devas were distressed and terrified, so they asked Sage Narada for some advice.

In the meantime, the innocent Sati had been reborn as Parvati, the daughter of Himavat, King of the Himalayas. In her new avatar, she was determined to marry Shiva, so she devoted very many years of penance and devotion dedicated to Shiva. During this time, she was known as Maa Brahmacharini.

Sage Narada witnessed the terror and destruction that menacing Tarakasura was causing. Feeling pity for the devas and other innocent beings, Narada decided to take some action. He travelled to the soaring snow-capped Himalayan mountains to find Parvati. Searching numerous steep mountain peaks, he eventually caught sight of a shimmering snowbank that had a majestic and awesome aura. Steadily approaching closer, Narada could immediately sense that an extremely powerful and divine being was situated here. He instantly recognised Parvati, sitting still in a lotus pose, chanting melodious mantras to attain her Lord Shiva. Large piles of thick frosty white snow encircled her from all sides. Narada praised her impressive devotion.

"Oh divine Parvati, your continuous devotion, contemplation and extreme efforts to Lord Shiva are truly commendable and praiseworthy. Your glory is sung throughout the whole world. My dear daughter, it is now time for you to know the truth about your past life. You are none other than innocent Sati reborn and you shall certainly fulfil your vow from your past life, you shall attain your heart's desire in this life. Your divine child with Shiva is destined to destroy the menacing Tarakasura and peace and balance will be restored once more." Sage Narada spoke with confidence. He continued to tell kind Parvati everything she needed to know about her past life and the reason for her current birth. Parvati's face lit up with a graceful wide smile, her eyes sparkled with delight, and she was overjoyed to hear about her successful destiny.

Parvati felt so empowered and inspired by Sage Narada. She continued to practice many more years of sincere devotion, spiritual practices and meditation to Shiva. The positive energy from her efforts was radiating all around her like a glowing halo of brilliance. With persuasion from the Kamadeva, Lord Shiva finally agreed to marry the devoted Parvati and they lived happily together on the majestic Mount Kailash, high in the Himalayas.

Combining their powerful energies, Shiva and Parvati made a mighty fiery seed. It was burning bright gold and full of immense energy. The seed was so radiant that Lord Agni, the god of fire, was given the responsibility to look after it but even he struggled with the brilliance and lustre. The luminous seed was given to the river goddess, Ganga, who safely transported it into a Saravana, a forest of reeds.

The dazzling seed was then given to six loving sisters known as Krittikas, named Śiva, Sambhūti, Prīti, Sannati, Anasūya and Kṣamā. They nurtured and cared for the wonderful seed which then transformed into a wonderful, charming, clever, strong boy. This brave son of Parvati and Shiva became known as Kartikeya because he was raised by these kind and doting Krittikas. He had six handsome and adoring faces, which were cared for by his six loving foster mothers.

From a young age, Kartikeya was a very inquisitive, intelligent and a spirited boy. He came to be known as Kumara. One day, he asked Lord Brahma, "What does the sacred syllable Om (Aum) represent?" Brahma was surprised to hear this question from such a young lad but replied in a very difficult riddle intending to confuse Kartikeya. To his surprise, clever Kartikeya understood everything perfectly! In a striking response, Kartikeya described the wonders of the sacred syllable Om in elegant poetry that even Brahma was astounded and felt humbled.

Soon after, the desperate devas visited young Kartikeya to ask him for his help. "Oh Kumara, you are just as strong as you are intelligent, please defend us against the evil tyrant, Tarakasura. Your bravery along with your superb martial arts and incredible warrior skills are perfect to help us," pleaded Indra, the King of the devas. Kartikeya was puzzled and replied, "I'm just a young lad, and you are supposed to be a powerful deva, how can I possibly defeat this asura?" Lord Indra clearly explained to Kartikeya, "Dear Murugan, only you are capable and skilled enough to defeat Tarakasura, even though you are just a youthful boy. You have superb strength and extraordinary intellect. You are immensely powerful as you are the divine son of Shiva and Parvati."

"Alright, I will help you," Kartikeya agreed. "Anything is possible with the blessings of my divine parents," he asserted. The devas blessed him with some mighty weapons. Parvati bestowed her son with a divine and unique weapon called a Vel. This slick and shiny javelin was a Shakti weapon, infused with divine strength which can swiftly destroy anything that it encounters. "Go my son, use your skills and courage to destroy the tyrant Tarakasura. May you be successful in restoring peace on Earth and the heavens once more. I bless you with victory, my dear Skanda."

With great confidence, armed with his mighty weapon and his mother's divine blessings, Skanda marched with an army, to find the menacing asura. "Tarakasura, you must stop terrorising innocent beings. If you do not make a wise choice to improve your behaviour, then you will face me in battle!" declared Skanda. A burst of loud laughter roared across the sky. "A pathetic little boy like you will never be able to destroy me!" taunted Tarakasura. "I am the son of the mighty Shiva and powerful Parvati. Your many years of causing suffering and distress will finally come to an end! You should accept your doom!" Skanda confidently announced.

Suddenly, remembering his boon, Tarakasura knew his life was in jeopardy. He felt nervous, his hands trembled with fear. "Could this be true? Could it be my end?" Out of fear, Tarakasura grabbed his huge mace and protective shield. Quickly gathering his large army, Tarakasura led a forceful charge towards the young Skanda, like a large herd of wildebeests racing through a small valley, trampling on everything in their path.

The battle commenced and Skanda swiftly and impressively defended himself with the powerful weapons gifted to him. They fought continuously for many days and nights. The battle was fierce, with swords slashing, gadas smashing and trishuls stabbing. Expert weapons were yielded by both sides. Skanda fought without breaking into a sweat, but Tarakasura was becoming weary. Soon after, Skanda carefully aimed his slick and sharp Vel weapon. With great strength, he thrust the celestial weapon across the scarred battlefield. His Vel pierced Tarakasura's evil chest, which destroyed the tyrant instantly. The sound of victory was declared as the crashing thud of his body fell to the ground, which shook vigorously.

The devas showered praise on Skanda as he gained victory! "You have bravely defeated the evil Tarakasura, we are extremely grateful to you for restoring peace and harmony." Indra rejoiced with relief. "Please give us the honour of joining us as a new deva. You can defend us and help to guard justice. It will be our privilege if you can join our team as the protector of devas. We will give you a new title as the God of War."

Parvati and Shiva were very impressed with Skanda and extremely proud of their dear son. They showered him with parental blessings. Skanda decided to take up his new position with the devas, and they were reassured. The world rejoiced as peace and balance were restored once again.

# MAA KATYAYANI

Meaning of name: Daughter of Sage Katyayana.

Mantra: Oṃ Devī Kātyāyanyai Namaḥ

Offering: Honey

Maa Katyayani is worshipped on the sixth day of Navratri. This form of Durga represents justice as she is the protector of good and Dharma. She is the warrior goddess and destroyer of evil which helps to maintain peace and harmony in the universe. Maa Katyayani symbolises courage, righteousness and compassion.

A long time ago, there lived a wise and learned sage named Katyayana. The intelligent sage was without a child but was desperate to be a father. "How I wish to have a young child of my own to cradle and look after," yearned Sage Katyayana. "I shall pray to the Trimurti. I will devote my meditation to Lord Brahma, Lord Vishnu and Lord Shiva. Hopefully, they can fulfil my wish to be a father," he decided with a hopeful heart. At once, Sage Katyayana sought to find a quiet and isolated place in a forest where he could meditate on the divine Trimurti. After many years of continuous prayers, the peaceful forest was echoing with Sanskrit chants, and an aura of positive energy enveloped the area where Sage Katyayana was meditating, which was glowing like soft moonlight.

During a similar time, the demonic Mahishasura was causing havoc and mayhem in the world. He was a large and powerful asura that could supernaturally transform his human appearance into a full-sized wild buffalo at any time. He had a boon that no man could kill him, which made Mahishasura very arrogant and selfish. He became threatening towards innocent beings. "I am invincible, there is no man in this entire world that can kill me! I can do plenty of evil deeds and there's no one to stop me!" Mahishasura exclaimed with a devilish laugh. He raided harmless people's homes and violently wounded anyone that got in his way. Eventually, Mahishasura claimed himself as the King. Everyone was too scared to take a stand against him so they reluctantly followed his wicked commands.

Many citizens were exhausted with Mahishasura's endless torments, so they began to desperately pray for help from the divine Trimurti. Having heard the prayers of these innocent beings, the Trimurti thought something must be done at once. Out of thin air, three divine beings majestically appeared in front of the people. "Mahishasura's doom is coming soon, there is a way to defeat the evil tyrant," the Trimurti reassured the innocent beings. "Just keep your faith, the slayer of Mahishasura will be here soon."

"We must act fast to protect these innocent and helpless people. The wicked Mahishasura has grown too arrogant and powerful, after having received a boon that no man can destroy him," stated Lord Vishnu to Lord Brahma and Lord Shiva. "He must be stopped, but we cannot destroy the villainous Mahishasura as he cannot be killed by any male form. Mahishasura's boon protects him," Lord Brahma responded. "We must combine all our powers and strength to create a being that is powerful enough to abolish maleficent Mahishasura," Lord Shiva suggested. The Trimurti all nodded their wise heads in agreement.

They assembled the other devas and stood unified in a mystical circle, divinely gathering all of their incredible energies. A brilliant and dazzling concentration of light appeared and shot up into the sky like a laser beam. When their incredible powers combined, all the colours of the rainbow fired out towards the ignited sky. The air struck with intense flashes of lightning and thunderous drums echoed in the atmosphere. The earth quaked and all the mountains rocked. Out of this radiance, a soft silhouette of an impressive figure slowly started to appear. Afterwards, the bright light began to soften slowly like a subtle sunset, from which a powerful and magnificent goddess appeared. This female was extremely fierce and radiant like a thousand shining suns. Her face gleamed with a graceful gentle smile. She had a strong and commanding presence, wearing a vibrant red saree which displayed confidence and strength. She adorned many mighty arms. A bold and ferocious lion could be seen behind her, which instantly and loyally obeyed her every command.

The Trimurti and devas offered their blessings to her. "Oh Divine Goddess Durga, you are worthy of infinite praise. You are the divine feminine force protecting goodness and justice, you are the bringer of peace and a guardian of Dharma. Please kindly go to defeat the tyrant Mahishasura as he is causing so much pain and suffering to innocent beings. Please protect the good and destroy the bad. Please restore peace and harmony so that Dharma may once again prevail," the Trimurti kindly requested.

Many devas gifted the gracious goddess with lots of powerful weapons to adorn her eighteen mighty hands. Shiva gave her a magnificent Trishul, Vishnu contributed a revolving chakra, Brahma provided a water-pot and a rosary, Varuna deva gave a conch shell, Agni deva gave a dangerous spear, Vaayu deva presented a flexible bow and two quivers full of arrows, Indra donated a dynamic thunderbolt and a bell from his loyal elephant, Yama deva gave her a staff weapon, Kubera gave a sturdy mace, Kaal awarded a sharp sword and shield, and Vishwakarma gave her a very brilliant battle-axe and impenetrable armour. The ocean gave her a garland of unfading lotuses and exquisite jewellery.

The glorious Goddess Durga was now armed and fully equipped to destroy the evil Mahishasura. "Oh Durga, we all bless you with victory to restore peace and harmony. When the time is right, you will be ready to fulfil your destiny, please bring an end to the maleficent Mahishasura," the devas proclaimed.

After some time, the Trimurti were drawn to the great admiration and dedication of Sage Katyayana. They discovered the bright aura in the forest and magically appeared there in an instant. "We are very impressed with your devotion Sage Katyayana, please ask us for a wish," they spoke graciously. "Oh my Lords, thank you for blessing me with your appearances, I am astounded that you are here! My heart yearns for a child, please can you bless me with this miracle? " Sage Katyayana humbly requested. "Your wish shall be granted, your daughter will be victorious and powerful. She will bring peace to the whole world!"

The magnificent goddess took the form of a beautiful newborn baby wrapped in a soft blanket, who was presented to Sage Katyayana. The newborn became known as Katyayani. Sage Katyayana looked after his daughter very lovingly as a truly dedicated father, with lots of warmth and love, they lived happily sharing many precious moments.

As she grew up to be a young child, Katyayani learned about material and spiritual knowledge and also became an expert in martial arts. Time passed quickly and Katyayani grew to be a clever, strong and wonderful adult. In his heart, Sage Katyayana knew that her life was meant for more. "My dearest daughter Katyayani, you are wise, learned, strong and powerful. You are ready to go and fulfil your destiny, to slay the evil villain asura Mahishasura," her father expressed proudly, but his heart was torn as he knew he now had to part with his dearest daughter. "With your kindness, guidance and blessings, I will be victorious!" Katyayani firmly reassured him. She gently hugged her dear father. "Thank you for all your love and support," she gratefully expressed, "I will make you proud".

Empowered by Sage Katyayana's blessings, her inner strength and self-confidence grew immensely. Katyayani ventured independently in search of the evil tyrant. On her journey, she came across a large city which looked like it had been ravaged by a monstrous beast. The houses looked tatty with wrecked windows and smashed doors as if they had been broken into and ransacked. The weak and weary people of the city looked like thin twigs which had been famished by hunger. They walked solemnly with their heads drooping down into their sunken shoulders as if their hopes and dreams were crushed. Katyayani could sense the presence of evil and oppression in the atmosphere. She could sense that monstrous Mahishasura was nearby.

In the distant town, Katyayani's intelligent eyes saw Mahishasura trampling on distressed innocent people like they were fallen leaves of an autumn tree. When she saw the panic-stricken faces of these harmless victims, Katyayani felt overwhelmed with compassion.

She bravely confronted Mahishasura. "You wicked Mahishasura! You have two choices. Please stop terrorising all these innocent people and allow them to live peacefully. If you do not, then you give me no choice but to fight you and bring an end to your evil ways. I want to preserve good and bring back peace and harmony," Katyayani firmly demanded.

The evil Mahishasura took one look at the young woman standing in front of him and bellowed an evil laugh. "HA! HA! HA! You cannot destroy me; I have a special boon that no man can kill me! You are not a worthy opponent but just a fragile woman! I will gladly have a battle with you. I can destroy you in less than a millisecond!" Mahishasura mocked deviously.

Katyayani mystically transformed into her original magnificent form, infused with the impressive Trimurti's strength and powers. Katyayani's eighteen mighty arms held divine and powerful weapons, she was wearing impenetrable protective armour, and she was mounted on her fearless and strong lion.

In this form, Katyayani stood valiantly. "You have a boon which protects you from a man. Mahishasura, you forget that I am a woman warrior! Be prepared to accept your doom!" she revealed with great confidence. Mahishasura became vexed and irritated. He immediately grabbed his bulky razor-sharp sword and shield and charged like a raging bull towards the female warrior goddess. The terrifying battle had commenced!

The fierce combat raged for nine days and nine nights, each day the battle intensified. Cunning Mahishasura ordered his huge army to attack Katyayani, ten soldiers at a time. These asuras hurled their innumerous metal spiked weapons at her. Maces clashed like the thunderous sound of crashing trucks. Swords slashed and clanged into each other. Thrashing weaponised arrows detonated like drone strikes. Mahishasura constantly changed between his human form and that of a furious, rampant buffalo with huge raging horns, the anger within him was at boiling point. He tried to bull charge Katyayani with intense force, but she was quick to shift away in defence. With her superior martial arts skills, Katyayani attacked her enemies with expertise and precision. Mahishasura hurled mountains against Katyayani by lifting them with his huge horns, but she pulverised them with a lethal shower of arrows.

On the tenth day, the demon Mahishasura was beginning to tire. His hand felt so heavy as if he was lifting a hundred volcanoes, his muscles were achy like they had been ripped apart, he fell to the ground with a big thud that shook the floor. It was time for Katyayani to fulfil her destiny. She mounted on her ferocious lion and commanded it to pounce on Mahishasura's fallen body, she then took one swift strike of her mighty sword, that destroyed the evil tyrant instantly.

The people rejoiced that evil Mahishasura had been destroyed and peace had returned once more. They gratefully praised Goddess Katyayani for restoring harmony and happiness. She became known as Mahishasuramardini, which means the "Slayer of Mahishasura."

## DAY SEVEN:
# MAA KAALRATRI

Meaning of name: "Kaal" means time and "Ratri" means night.

Mantra: Oṃ Devī Kālarātryai Namaḥ

Offering: Jaggery-unrefined sugar.

On the seventh day of Navratri, Maa Kaalratri is worshipped. She is also known as Maa Kaali (also spelled as Kali). "Kaal" means time and "Ratri" means night. Maa Kaalratri is fearless and heroic as she fights to bring an end to injustice. Maa Kaalratri is the destroyer of evil and harmful energies. She is the fiercest form of Goddess Durga. She symbolises intense strength, resilience, skill, endurance, efficiency and empathy.

Long long ago, Maa Katyayani destroyed the evil demon Mahishasura and brought back peace and harmony to the world. Having heard about the death of their friend, two asuras named Chanda and Munda were conjuring up an evil plan. "Mahishasura is no more, it is now up to us to cause havoc and mayhem in the world. Let people now bow to us and see our power, we can be rulers!" the two villains gruffed. "Let us go and terrorise the devas, we can invade Indra's kingdom, Devalok, and steal all their valuable wealth," plotted Chanda. "I want Indra's blood as revenge for killing Mahishasura, our dear friend. I will not rest until I get payback!" Munda declared with deep piercing red angry eyes.

"Sweet revenge
will be sure to
happen as we have the
special boons that no man
or deva can destroy us. Indra
will be begging for mercy at our feet
in an instant!" Chanda comforted him,
placing his hand on Munda's broad
shoulder. They looked at each other with hateful
eyes, determined to cause misery and suffering to
anyone and everyone that crossed their path.

The two asuras gathered their mighty weapons, assembled a great brawny army and launched a fierce surprise attack on Devalok. Indra and the other devas fled in fear to the high Himalayan mountains, desperately in search of Lord Shiva's help.

"Oh Lord Shiva, please save me from these asuras. They have ruined peace and harmony once again. Chanda and Munda have vowed to kill me. They are accompanied by other devilish and powerful thugs, including Raktabeeja. Please do something, my Lord Shiva!" pleaded distraught and desperate Indra.

"These asuras have a special boon that they cannot be destroyed by a man. You should ask Parvati for help," guided Lord Shiva. The devas hoped that Parvati would hold the answers to defeat the evil asuras. "Dear Divine Mother Parvati, please help us for we have nowhere else to turn. You are our only hope to end this terror upon good beings, these asuras are ready to destroy everything!" The devas begged Parvati. Having witnessed the fear and worry of the devas, compassionate Parvati quickly agreed to assist them.

The gentle Parvati conjured a magnificent warrior Goddess named Chandi. She was fierce and fearless. Her complexion was as black as the night's sky. She adorned many mighty arms holding formidable weapons such as a flashy thunderbolt, a terrifying trishul and a razor-sharp sword. Her matted hair adorned a crescent moon symbolising her mastery of time. She wore a garland of skulls and serpents, and she was seated on a ferocious lion. Chandi was ready to fight the evil tyrants and bring back peace and harmony.

Catching sight of the formidable and fierce Goddess Chandi, the asura army started to tremble with fear. "Stop your terrorising of these good beings, and you shall be forgiven for your bad deeds. Otherwise, you will have to face the fatal consequences," Goddess Chandi warned the asuras with great courage and conviction in her demands.

"You are no match for us, the mighty asuras! You are just a feeble woman, we will destroy you at once!" Chanda and Munda angrily commanded. The two tyrants gathered their most destructive weapons and together charged toward Chandi at the same time, launching a fierce double attack. This unfair ambush made Chandi extremely enraged, and she became even more frightening in her manner and appearance. Munda slashed his jagged sword at her trusted lion which let out an earth-shattering fuming roar. Overcome with compassion and the need for justice, Chandi was unstoppable and instantly destroyed Munda with a thrash of her mighty thunderbolt. Chanda saw the death of his friend and was filled with even more anger and hatred. He mercilessly attacked Chandi but she quickly readied her terrifying trishul to point towards her enemy, which destroyed him immediately. Having slain Chanda and Munda, she became known as 'Chamunda'.

The asura army general raced frantically to find his asura friend, Raktabeeja. "Chanda and Munda have been slain by a fierce woman warrior. She is single-handedly nearly destroying the whole asura army. You must do something Raktabeeja!" begged the scared asura general, from fear of what he had just seen. "This menacing woman is no match for me. I have special powers that from even a single drop of my mighty blood, I can multiply and many more powerful Raktabeeja's will appear. It is impossible to destroy me!" announced Raktabeeja arrogantly. "From my blood, there will be thousands of Raktabeeja's ready to end her!"

Determined to destroy her, Raktabeeja marched tensely towards Chandi, the ground quaked beneath his huge body as he stomped to the battleground. The two fierce and frightening warriors, raging Raktabeeja and valiant Chandi stood opposite, aiming deadly stares.

"HA HA HA," Raktabeeja roared a wicked laugh. "Is that it? You are my enemy?! I will destroy you in no time. You are no match for me, for my name is Raktabee-ja! Rakta means blood and Beeja means seed. For every drop of blood that falls from my mighty body, it will act as a seed and I will be cloned that many more times! I am impossible to defeat!" he claimed. "How can one woman defeat countless multiples of me?!"

Chandi knew that her new enemy was filled with extreme arrogance, full of ravaging hatred and he was pure evil. With all her might and power, she breathtakingly transformed herself into an even more terrifying form to intimidate Raktabeeja. Her pitch-black deadly gaze became even more lethal. Eyes as black as midnight, her strong weapons renewed with even more dangerous might. In one of her arms, she now carried the skull of an evil asura, which she held in the form of a hollow bowl. She became the form of Maa Kaalratri, the Goddess powerful enough to devour even time itself.

Raktabeeja let out a chilling roar and darted towards Kaalratri, swinging his daunting monstrous sword. She swiftly moved away and retaliated by using her weapons to strike her attacker. Her razor-sharp sword struck Raktabeeja's arm, and several drops of his evil blood fell to the ground. A few seconds later, these drops of blood sprouted exact duplicates of Raktabeeja and soon there were many tyrannical enemies, which became a stronger army in battle. Upon seeing this, Kaalratri quickly used a skull that she was holding as a bowl and hurriedly collected any blood droplets as they fell towards the floor to stop any droplets from reaching the ground and resprouting. Kaalratri now had many Raktabeejas' to fight, and they were simultaneously viciously attacking her. She had to become equally destructive and ferocious if she were to destroy the multiple demons, so she used her powerful energies to strike at her enemy. Raktabeeja's burgundy blood was oozing out of his terrifying body, Kaalratri desperately tried to collect it so that it didn't reach the floor but her blood collecting skull bowl was now full to the top.

She had to act superfast in that moment, she drank the blood droplets before they could reach the floor so it would be impossible for there to be more clones of Raktabeeja. The gruelling and fierce battle continued and Raktabeeja was beginning to tire because he could not clone himself any longer, as his blood was caught before it could reach the ground and could not duplicate again. With a mighty swing of her sword, Kaalratri eventually destroyed the evil Raktabeeja.

Even after killing her enemy, Kaalratri was so full of ferocious energy that she could not be calmed down. The devas were frightened by her fierce form, and they approached Lord Shiva. "Having transformed into the fierce forms of Chandi, Chamunda and Kaalratri, Parvati was successful in destroying Raktabeeja, Chanda and Munda and many other evil asuras. She has eliminated the dangers. Now you must help her to calm down and transform back into peaceful Parvati again. Please help us, Shiva, for only you can help here My Lord," Indra requested. "We are scared of what she might do next."

Shiva graciously nodded his head and agreed to assist. He mystically appeared on the battlefield where Kaalratri had destroyed the wicked asuras. The battlefield was littered with lifeless bodies scattered on a large carpet of crimson blood. Shiva tried to talk to Kaalratri but she was still enraged, she was unable to listen. He knelt down showing full respect in front of her, but she did not see him and accidentally stepped on him. Having realised her mistake and overcome with guilt, Kaalratri bit her tongue. She instantly helped her husband to get up from the floor by lending a helpful hand. She apologised to Shiva and regained her form as tranquil and peaceful Parvati.

She was praised by all for her quick-witted actions and strength to destroy the evil tyrants that no man was capable of undertaking this task. Peace and balance were regained.

# MAA MAHAGAURI

Meaning of name: "Maha" means great, "Gauri" means radiant or fair
Mantra: Oṃ Devī Mahāgauryai Namaḥ
Offering: Coconut.

On the eighth day of Navratri, Maa Mahagauri is worshipped. Mahagauri is made up of two Sanskrit words, "Maha" means great and "Gauri" means radiant or fair. She is brilliant and protects the good. Mahagauri helps spiritual seekers and guides them towards release in the cycle of rebirth, by granting salvation. She has the power to inspire and fulfil the heart's desire of her devotees. She is also known as "Kaushiki" as she comes from Parvati. She symbolises intelligence, innovation and flexibility.

A long time ago, Shumbha and Nishumbha were two very powerful asuras. They were very strong but unfortunately, decided to use their strength to torment and terrorise innocent people. "I will break your necks if you do not worship us. I will destroy your murti's of Vishnu and your shivlings! No more Vishnu, no more Shiva! From now on, you pray to us and no one else! " Shumbha ordered. "If I see anyone praying to other deities apart from us, we will make you suffer! Shumbha and Nishumbha are your Gods from now on!" Nishumbha threatened as he waved his huge sharp axe.

The civilians were frightened but they had no choice, and certainly did not want to meet the fate of that axe. They were forced to worship Shumbha and Nishumbha against their wishes, and those who tried to stand up to the two terrible tyrants were killed. "We are undefeatable!" they both laughed wickedly as they wreaked havoc upon the lives of innocent people.

The vulnerable people were seized as slaves and often beaten, scolded and tormented with lashing whips and long slender canes, the asuras were out of control. They could not take it any longer! "Devi Durga, please come to our aid. You have already saved so many in the past, in your magnificent form of Maa Kaalratri and Maa Chamunda. Please save us too!" The desperate citizens prayed with all their love and devotion. Overcome with compassion and kindness, Maa Kaalratri mystically appeared before them. "My dear devotees, do not worry. Shumbha and Nishumbha's dooms are nearby. They will not cause you any more fear or torment. Mahagauri will be created to destroy them. In this form, I will destroy these two tyrants and bring back peace and serenity," she softly reassured them.

At that moment, using some of her own skin, Maa Kaalratri sculpted a new goddess. Maa Kaalratri's original dark raven skin had transformed into a glowing soft fair complexion like a jasmine flower. Her matted hair became soft and silky which flowed like a satin drape. She adorned an elegant golden crown which glistened with rubies and diamonds as it caught the sun's mystical rays. Instead of adorning a scary skull garland, the new goddess was wearing a fragrant flower necklace which smelt like fresh roses. She wore a beautiful pearly white saree that had sparkling precious gemstones as decorations. Intricate bangles adorned her soft and gentle hands, and exquisite anklets jingled on her feet as the newly formed goddess walked with great confidence. "My dear devotees, I will save you from these two tyrants in my form as Mahagauri," she asserted with a gentle pleasing smile that instantly eased the worries and anxieties of her devotees.

The splendour of a hundred suns that encircled Mahagauri, caught the attention of the two villains. "What is this lustre that attracts me like a honeybee to the sweet nectar of a perfumed white rose? Whatever it is, I desire to have it, now!" commanded Shumba ravenously. "Let's grab it, brother. For everything is ours to seize!" exclaimed fiendish Nishumbha. Off they hurried, their immoral eyes full of greed and raging uncontrollable desire.

As they approached closer to the radiant sphere, they froze like ice statues as soon as they caught sight of the magnificent and beautiful Mahagauri. Completely awes truck in her presence, they stared for several minutes like gaping gulls. Their evil minds were filled with irresistible cravings to marry her. "Oh beautiful lady, I will marry you this instant! Come with me, you are mine now." proclaimed Shumbha with a deep intimidating voice. "I will take you because everything in this kingdom belongs to me!"

"Hmm, you wish to capture me and expect me to be your slave? I do not think so. Your marriage proposals really need some practice. Are you as pathetic as your advances?" Mahagauri chuckled as she mocked Shumbha. Having heard these insults, Nishumbha was enraged. "How dare you speak to my brother like that! I will kidnap you in a flash and keep you imprisoned as our most prized hostage!"

"Hmm," Mahagauri softly sniggered. "You are both even more wretched than I thought. You have no right to kidnap any innocent lady or person, and you will certainly not attain me in that way!" she angrily replied. "However, I have a better proposal for you. If either of you can defeat me in battle, then I will marry you willingly. Do we have a deal?" suggested Mahagauri, with a cheeky smile.

A loud roar of evil laughter echoed throughout the sky above like a distressed thunderclap. "You might as well marry me now, beautiful lady. I can defeat you quicker than a flash of lightning!" tormented Nishumbha.

The two demonic asuras called upon their large army to gather instantly. Nishumbha was placed at the front of the humongous asura army, closely shadowed by his tyrant brother Shumbha. Beholding their dangerous weapons, grinning at Mahagauri who stood opposite them, alone. The battle was ready to start at any moment.

Mahagauri mystically transformed into Kali once again, which startled Shumbha and Nishumbha. Now adorned with formidable weapons, in her fiercest form and ready for battle, she eagerly anticipated the first move by the asura army.

"Soldiers, capture this weak woman!" Nishumbha commanded. "CHARGE!" The hefty asura army led a furious ambush on the goddess, who skilfully and courageously retaliated with equal force. Shumbha and Nishumbha rained a turbulent storm of arrows towards her, Kali quickly split all the arrows that were shot by the asuras. Kali's arms swayed with great might, her sharp sword, incising axe and piercing trishul slew many asuras simultaneously.

Nishumbha grasped his sharp sword along with a shiny shield and struck the Goddess's lion on the head. Kali quickly raced to defend her trusted and loyal ally by cutting Nishumbha's sword and shield with a sharp-edged arrow. Nishumbha hurled his spear, but with the blow of her mighty fist, it turned into dust. Her fierce eyes targeted Nishumbha, and she swiftly hurled a dart which pierced his heart. Another powerful asura emerged from Nishumbha's slain body, which stormed towards the Goddess. Within seconds she destroyed the evil asura with her unstoppable blade.

Extremely furious by the death of his brother, Shumbha led a vicious battle charge like a thousand meteors crashing to Earth. The ground trembled as destruction was imminent. Swiftly responding, Kali called upon the female counterparts of the Trimurti; Brahmaani (Sarasvati, wife of Brahma), Vaishnavi (Lakshmi, wife of Vishnu), and Shivani (Parvati, wife of Shiva). They all gathered their weapons and helped to fight against the large asura army. Brahmaani repulsed the asuras by the sprinkling of holy and purified water. Vaishnavi used her impressive chakra to eliminate them and Shivani pierced the enemy with her trishul.

Kali was determined to find Shumbha. He deviously attacked her from behind with a sturdy swing of his mace. Kali's divine sharp arrows split his mace into symmetrical halves which further infuriated Shubha. She lifted him up and flung him in the air, Shumbha whirled like a tornado before crashing to the floor.

The evil-natured Shumbha raised his fist and hastily rushed forward like a fireball, desiring to destroy Kali. Having seen Shumbha's violent charge, Kali pierced him on his arrogant chest with a dangerous dart, which threw him down to the earth. The ground trembled and the seas surged. Having seen Shumbha's life less bulky body, the rest of the asura troops cowardly ran away from the battlefield. Victory belonged to the brave Goddesses.

The universe became happy again and regained perfect peace. The previously flaming clouds calmed and cooled, the flooded rivers flowed gently once more, and the raging red sky grew clear with a sapphire glow. The sun blazed with brilliance and tranquillity filled the air.

The hearts and minds of the devas and people became overjoyed. "We are eternally grateful to you, thank you for freeing this world of evil. We can now live in peace," praised the innocent people. Kali smiled gently and raised her right hand open palmed hand, showering her blessings on them.

She then left to travel to Mansarovar lake in the Himalayas. Kali immersed herself in the serene lake and elegantly transformed into the graceful form of Mahagauri.

# MAA SIDDHIDATRI

Meaning of name: "Siddhi" means supernatural power and "Datri" means giver.

Mantra: Oṃ Devī Siddhidātryai Namaḥ

Offering: Sesame seeds.


Maa Siddhidatri is worshipped on the ninth day of Navratri. This form of Durga fulfils hopes and dreams. Her name consists of two Sanskrit words; "Siddhi" which means supernatural power and "Datri" means giver. Maa Siddhidatri blesses her devotees with wisdom and awards them with spiritual knowledge. She is the destroyer of ignorance and giver of eternal peace.

When time, space and the universe were non-existent, everything was blank. Only a void of emptiness, there was simply nothing. Not even a minuscule sound or light existed, only complete silence and darkness enveloped everything. Time was nowhere to be found. Suddenly, a glorious and brilliant light emerged which shone in all directions with a blazing brightness that instantly illuminated everywhere. Soon, the dazzling light softened into various mystical waves and countless colours. Out of this wonderful brilliance, a magical silhouette of a divine lady appeared, it was Maa Kushmanda. Taking a glance around her, she knew she had a very important mission, which was to create the universe and the whole of existence. By the grace of her miraculous smile, Maa Kushmanda created three divine figures, Mahasaraswati, Mahalakshmi and Mahakali.

"You are my three divine creations. You come from my divinity and hence you are also spiritual and sacred. You will carry on creating by sculpting and styling my celestial energy so that it can create, preserve and renew the entire universe," Maa Kushmanda gently announced with a radiant smile.

The three equally magnificent creations from Maa Kushmanda's divine shakti, each continued the craft of creation. The body of Mahakali gave birth to a male named Shiva, and a female, Saraswati. Similarly, Mahalakshmi also gave birth to a male named Brahma and a female called Lakshmi. Maa Kushmanda then glanced at Mahasaraswati, who then gave birth to a male, Vishnu, and a female, Parvati.

"Welcome Brahma, Vishnu and Shiva. Each of you will be tasked with significant roles and you must fulfil these roles to the best of your ability. Brahma shall create. Vishnu will take charge of the preservation of the universe and Shiva will help with destroying the old so renewal can take place," Maa Kushmanda stated to the newly formed Trimurti.

Confused at her wish, the Trimurti looked at each other with puzzled faces. "Oh divine Goddess, we need some help to do this. Kindly bless us with siddhis, supernatural powers!" requested Brahma. "So be it," she replied.

At that moment, Maa Kushmanda magically transformed herself into Maa Siddhidatri. She glowed with a calming sky-blue aura as she sat elegantly on a pure pale pink lotus flower. "I will bless you with my very own Shakti, powers and strength. These siddhis, supernatural powers will always be with you and support you with your roles," she approved with a gentle smile.

Maa Siddhidatri kindly raised her right hand up to her right shoulder and opened her palm to face the Trimurti and the Goddesses. Suddenly a flash of dynamic energy came from the centre of her palm, which was divided into six equal segments. Her positive energy, divine miraculous powers and siddhis were transferred to them as they all developed a divine splendour. The Trimurti and Goddesses shone like a thousand suns, as they radiated with divine siddhis. Halos of soft divine light encircled them.

They were now blessed with Ashtasiddhis, eight supernatural powers. These are:

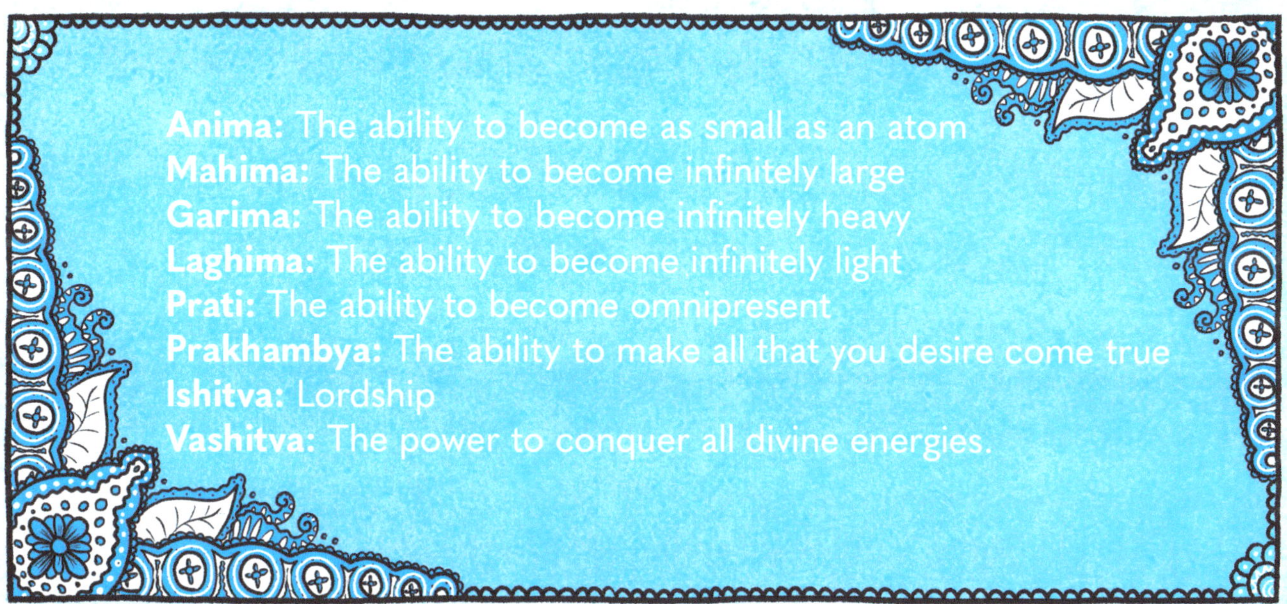


Maa Siddhidatri ingeniously offered companions to her wonderful and miraculous creations, so that their skills and talents are suitably matched. Saraswati was paired with Brahma; Lakshmi was matched with Vishnu and Parvati was complemented by Shiva.

I have blessed you with many siddhis. Brahma, you can now use these supernatural powers and energies to create the universe," she requested softly. Puzzled Brahma felt overwhelmed and worried at the thought of such a huge daunting task. "Oh, divine Goddess! Thank you for your kindness, compassion, and blessings of many siddhis. Although I must admit that I am feeling very anxious as I do not know where to begin with this monumental task! I require both masculine and feminine strengths. I need your help, please guide me, Divine Mother!" Lord Brahma requested Maa Siddhidatri.

"Fear not, I will help you with Shiva's assistance," she kindly responded. On hearing Lord Brahma's request, Maa Siddhidatri gently nodded to Lord Shiva and he telepathically understood the Goddess's request. In the spur of the moment, Lord Parvati and Lord Shiva who were standing side by side, carefully took a small sidestep towards each other. There was a magnificent glow from the swirling stardust that swished around them. Miraculously appearing from the dazzling brilliance was a vertical left half of Lord Shiva and right half of Maa Parvati.

Awestruck with the elegance and ingenuity of Maa Siddhidatri, Brahma knelt down in reverence and respect with his palms joined. "Dear Ardhanarishvara, I show my gratitude to you by bowing down at your divine feet," Brahma prayed. This ardha form of half goddess and half god is truly inspirational. Just as a bird needs two wings to fly successfully, creation will also be infused with both masculine and feminine energies. Thank you for guiding me and giving me the confidence to create the rest of the universe!"

Lord Brahma spoke in admiration. He gazed at Maa Siddhidatri and acknowledged, " You are the creator of every particle in the universe and the whole of existence. You are various types of matter from regular matter to antimatter, dark matter and degenerate matter. Your energy will be infused within the whole of creation, and it will be a base in which the cosmos is formed, just like how paint sits on a canvas. Thank you Maa Siddhidatri."

With a compassionate smile, Maa Siddhidatri blessed the Gods and Goddesses with ten more siddhis. Embodied with these supernatural powers, the magnificent six were now ready to fulfil their divine duties for the entire universe.

# A Sanskrit Shloka Dedicated To Mother Durga

## Sanskrit

सर्वमङ्गलमाङ्गल्ये शिवे सर्वार्थसाधिके ।

शरण्ये त्र्यम्बके गौरि नारायणि नमोऽस्तु ते ॥

## Transcript

sarvamangalamāngalye shive sarvārthasādhike |

sharanye tryambake gauri nārāyani namo'stu te ||

## Meaning

O Divine Mother, who brings auspiciousness to all,

the equal to Lord Shiva, the giver of divine energy and the One who helps people to achieve,

the One who protects like a mother, the all-seeing with a third spiritual eye,

O Divine Mother, I humbly seek your blessings.

# Weapons of Goddess Durga Gifted By:

**Trishul (Trident)** - Lord Shiva
Symbolises: The three qualities:
sattva (goodness), rajas (passion), tamas (inertia).

**Sudarshan Chakra (Disc)** - Lord Vishnu
Symbolises: The centre of creation.

**Thunderbolt and Bell** - Lord Indra
Symbolises: Firmness of character, determination
and focus.

**Bow and Arrow** - Vayu Dev
Symbolises: The combination of powers
symbolises energy.

**Spear** - Agni Dev
Symbolism: One pointed devotion and ambition.
Broadening of the mind with true knowledge.

**Shankh (Conch)** - Varuna Dev
Symbolises: The sound of creation, Aum.

**Kamandal (water pot) and Mala (rosary)** - Lord Brahma
Symbolises: Kamandal represents the elixir of life (amrit).
Mala represents our connection to the Divine.

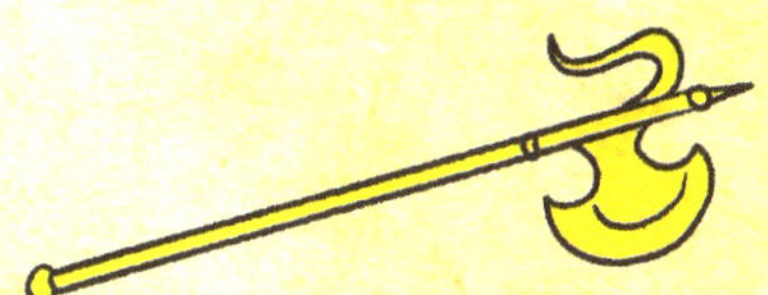

**Battle Axe and Armour** - Vishwakarma
Symbolises: The powers of Vishwakarma, the power to
destroy as well as create.

**Staff Weapon** - Yama
Symbolises: Creative energy.

**Gada (mace)** - Kubera
Symbolises: Strength and power.

**Sword and Shield** - Kaal
Symbolises: Intellect and wisdom, this weapon is usually
carried by people who have a sense of responsibility and
the understanding to know right from wrong.

# Glossary

Agni deva - God of fire.

Anima - the ability to become as small as an atom. A supernatural power (siddhi).

Ardha - half.

Ardhanarishvara - a divine form which has a vertical left half of Lord Shiva and right half of Maa Parvati.

Ashtasiddhis - eight supernatural powers.

Asura - demon like character.

Aum - a sacred Hindu symbol which represents God and the entire Universe. Alternative spelling is Om.

Auspicious - success, good luck, hope.

Avatar - incarnation.

Beeja - seed.

Brahma - God of creation, part of the Trimurti.

Brahmaani - Sarasvati, wife of Brahma.

Brahmachari - a male monk. Referred to as Shiva in this book.

Brahmacharini - a female monk. Referred to as Parvati in this book.

Chamunda - the destroyer of Chanda and Munda. Another name for Durga.

Chakra - discus. A powerful weapon with a serrated edge.

Chandra - moon.

Devalok - Indra's kingdom. A place where celestial beings and chief Vedic Gods live.

Devas - divine celestial beings, a chief Vedic god responsible for natural and moral order in the cosmos.

Dharma - cosmic law, duty, righteousness.

Dhatri - giver.

Gada - mace.

Garima - the ability to become infinitely heavy. A supernatural power (siddhi).

Gauri - radiant or fair.

Ghanta - bell.

Indra - the leader of devas. God of Rain.

Ishitva - Lordship. A supernatural power (siddhi).

Ishvara - Lord, God.

Kaal - God of time.

Kamadeva - God of love and desire.

Kamandal - a water pot.

Kartikeya - first-born child of Shiva and Parvati.

Kaushiki - one that comes from Parvati. Another name of Mahagauri.

Kubera - God of wealth.

Laghima - The ability to become infinitely light. A supernatural power (siddhi).

Maa - mother

Maha - great.

Maha Shivaratri - a festival dedicated to Lord Shiva and Parvati.

Mahima - the ability to become infinitely large. A supernatural power (siddhi).

Mahishasuramardini - slayer of Mahishasura. Another name for Durga.

Mala - beaded necklace, rosary.

Mandap - wedding canopy where a Hindu marriage ceremony takes place.

Mata - mother.

Murugan - first-born child of Shiva and Parvati.

Navdurga - the nine forms of Durga.

Om - a sacred Hindu symbol which represents God and the entire universe. Alternative spelling is Aum.

Penance - difficult spiritual disciplines undertaken. Also known as Tapasya.

Prakhambya - the ability to make all that you desire come true. A supernatural power (siddhi).

Prati - the ability to become omnipresent. A supernatural power (siddhi).

Quiver - a container for holding arrows.

Rajas - a quality of passion.

Rakta - blood.

Raktabeeja - an asura that was defeated by Maa Kaalratri.

Rudraksha beads - prayer beads associated with Lord Shiva.

Saravana - a forest of reeds.

Satva - a quality of goodness.

Shailaputri - the daughter of the mountains.

Shakti - strength, power, might.

Shiva - God of renewal and destroyer. Part of the Trimurti.

Shivani - Parvati, wife of Shiva. Also known as Maheshwari.

Shivling - a symbol of Shiva.

Shwetambardhara - one who is dressed in white clothes. Another name of Mahagauri.

Siddhi - supernatural powers.

Skanda - first-born child of Shiva and Parvati.

Staff weapon - a long pole weapon.

Sudarshan Chakra - a discus that belongs to Lord Vishnu.

Surya deva - Sun God.

Tamas - a quality of inertia and dullness.

Tapas - austere spiritual practices such as fasting, staying in a fixed posture for a long time, meditation.

Trimurti -  trinity of Hindu Gods. Brahma, Vishnu and Shiva.

Trishul - trident.

Tunic - a loose garment that is usually sleeveless and reaching to the knees.

Vaayu deva - God of the wind.

Vaishnavi - Lakshmi, wife of Vishnu.

Varuna deva - God of the seas and oceans.

Vashitva - the power to conquer all. A supernatural power (siddhi).

Vel - slick and shiny javelin, Skanda's weapon.

Vishnu - God of preservation, part of Trimurti, husband of Lakshmi.

Vishwakarma - God of craftsmanship and architecture.

Yagna -  ritual to the divine that is conducted in front of a sacred fire.

Yama - God of death.

# About the Authors and Illustrator

## Asmita Bhudia BSc (Hons) PGCE

Asmita has been a qualified teacher since 2007 and has been teaching in UK schools as a professional teacher, experienced in working in both primary and secondary schools.

Asmita has been voluntarily running Hinduism classes for children on a weekly basis since 2007 (and continues to do so) to promote the wonderful teachings of Sanatana Dharma (Hinduism). She also volunteers as a key member for Hindu Education Board UK which helps to promote Hinduism in UK schools.

Asmita is the mother of twin girls. She currently teaches Sanskrit in a primary school.

## Sunita Shah BSc (Hons)

Sunita is the mother of two boys, and the creator of, "The Jai Jais" series, which was established in 2015. Her boys inspired her to develop The Jai Jais. She wanted the next generation to connect with their religious and cultural heritage in a modern and engaging way.

Sunita has been a practising speech and language therapist for over 20 years.  She has worked as a clinical lead in a senior role within the NHS for 20 years.  Sunita now works independently with her private practice "Together Let's Communicate", which has been established for 15 years www.tlc-speechtherapy.co.uk.

## James Ballance, BA (Hons) Illustration with Animation, UWE

James has worked on various projects including animation, computer games, advertising, and children's books. After moving from Devon to London he worked in a special needs school where he made the connection with Sunita. www.jamesballance.myportfolio.com

Other products available in The Jai Jais range...

**The Jai Jais App**
Free download available on iOS and Android.
Includes calendar, flash cards of gods and goddesses, and Ebooks.

**Baby Board Books**
**0-2 years**
Shiva
Krishna
Lakshmi
Durga
Hanuman
Ganesh

**Primary Series**
**2-4 years**

| | |
|---|---|
| Shiva | Rama |
| Krishna | Saraswati |
| Lakshmi | Kali Ma |
| Durga | Ganga Ma |
| Hanuman | Vishnu |
| Ganesh | Brahma |

**Festival Series**
**4-6 years**
Diwali
Holi
Mahavir

**Legends Series**
**6+**
Ramayana
Hanuman Chalisa For Children
The 10 Avatars of Vishnu
Nine Divine Goddesses of Navratri

*Ages are recommendations only.

Head to our website or follow us on social media for more details.

www.thejaijais.com